Multiplying Model
Pastor-Initiated Church Planting

By James R. Beller

PRAIRIE FIRE PRESS
Arnold ♦ St. Louis, Missouri

Please visit multiplyingmodel.com, the place where pastors, church planters and evangelists can connect to make the model work.

Table of Contents

PART 1
The Model Defined

Chapter 1
Think With Me

Set aside your preconceived notions. In order to use the principles of this book you will have to do some thinking. There is quite a bit of talk in and about the independent Baptist world about church planting. The rediscovery of the important work of church planting is good for the whole country. Our purpose is to share a different kind of model, one that has proven to be uniquely successful and unquestionably scriptural.

After prayer and much prodding by other preachers, we have decided to put the principles of the Separate Baptist church planting model on paper. Our hope is a general return to this model, sorely needed in these last days.

This book is somewhat a compilation of presentations and messages preached in conferences in several states over the last few years. The three most prominent were: the October 9-10, 2008 missions conference at Pacific Baptist Church—Long Beach, California, Pastor Joe Esposito; the March 9-11, 2009 Buckeye Baptist Fellowship held at Lighthouse Baptist Church—Sandusky, Ohio, Pastor Richard Mick moderator, and the June 8-9, 2009 North American Church Planting Conference at Liberty Baptist Church—Toledo, Ohio, Pastor Rick Rust.

The information contained here is designed **for established pastors who have a burden to plant a church from their existing church**. An evangelist will greatly benefit from this information as well, if he desires to do what the Apostle Paul referred to as "the work of an evangelist." We find that the biblical and historical role of the evangelist ought to be discussed. In addition, the man who believes he is called to start or plant a church will receive a new perspective on how this most important work is accomplished.

The Multiplying Model does NOT advocate:
   1. Branching, or dismissing members of your church to start another church. You will not lose members of your church if you use this model.
   2. Missionary fund raising. In fact, you should plan to start

1

another church with very little money.
   3. Team missions. Paul's missionary team, except for those
      that *sat as a church,* consisted of himself and one other
      person.
   4. College led efforts.
   5. A group of churches banding together to plant a church.
   **6. A single meeting or week of meetings that results in a
      church plant.**
   7. Isolated outpost missions. The isolated model may have
      to be used in remote places, but not too often in America.
   8. We are not teaching foreign missions either, although the
      principles shared could be used on the foreign field once
      the first church is established.

The Multiplying Model DOES advocate:
   1. Pastor-initiated church planting.
   2. Churches literally planting a new church.
   3. The established pastor finding a man for the new work
      while he is in the process of planting and pastoring the
      new work himself.
   **4. A pastor and his established church coming alongside a
      planter of a new work.**
   **5. The evangelist, pastor and new church planter working
      together for greater success.**

See the difference? Let us establish some definitions right away:

   Jerusalem: The area within reasonable immediate reach of an
established church and pastor.
   Judaea: The area out of reasonable immediate reach of the
established church and pastor, but within reach of a church plant
from the established church. This might be 30-40 minutes away up
to two hours away.
   Samaria and the Uttermost parts: The area out of reasonable
immediate reach and therefore out of reach for a church plant
using the model in this study. Samaria and the Uttermost parts
require a sending out, or apostolic model, what is commonly

2

termed *missions*. This book concentrates on Judaea, (see Matthew 28:19-20) but a missionary doing the work of an evangelist could use this model for greater success after the first church is planted on the field.

Evangelist: New Testament preacher, someone who preaches the Gospel and gathers converts into existing or new churches.

The established pastor: This is the man whom God often burdens to plant new churches within his Judaea. He is a pastor, doing the work of an evangelist. He will be the pastor of the new church plant until God sends the new pastor. Notice Paul's behavior at Ephesus: **"Therefore watch, and remember, that by the space of three years I ceased not to warn every one night and day with tears."**—Acts 20:31. Paul was an evangelist in the office of a pastor, continuing the work of an evangelist for three years.

The sowing church: The church from which the established pastor launches the new church.

The new or budding church: People attending the meetings of the church plant before it is publically constituted. If a convert is baptized during this time, he is a member of the sowing church until the constituting of the new church. At that time he is dismissed from the sowing church into the new church. This we learned from experience and believe it is the correct order.

The new pastor: This is the man God sends to take charge of the church plant in whatever stage it has progressed.

Absolute death: When a church dies and has not reproduced itself in the planting of new churches, we term this *absolute death*.

Four Factors of Success with the Model

This church planting model will fail for lack of any of the following factors:

    1. Strong pastoral leadership. The pastor of the sowing church must bear the pain in the beginning. He must bear that pain alone without complaint and with patience. The sowing church members cannot know this pain from the mouth of the pastor. When they see his efforts, they will naturally follow their pastor.

2. **Participation by the sowing church membership**. The majority ought to participate in visitation, *grocery supply*, building provision and *sitting as a church*.
3. **The right man to pastor the new work.** He has to be called to that location not by convenience nor arbitrarily, but by divine design.
4. **The right location.** The exact place of God's choosing.

The church planting model of the Separates will fail for lack of any of the above factors. When the ministry of a bona-fide evangelist is added to the effort the rate of success is greatly enhanced.

When you become armed with the knowledge of the scriptures and the testimony of your forefathers, may God lay upon your heart some Judea. May God bring to fruition churches for the sake of our country, our children and our children's children.

Chapter 2
Defining the Model

Seven Unique Characteristics of the Separate Baptist Model
1. Churches planted churches.
2. Pastors initiated the new works.
3. Pastors preached and pastored in multiple places.
4. Evangelists were chiefly church planters.
5. Pastors were evangelists and evangelists did pastoral work.
6. Little or no money was needed.
7. The sowing church would *sit as a church*.

What could happen if this model is used?

These principles and ideas were gleaned from the process of researching, writing and carrying out the will of God for our church.

We do not pretend that this is the final authority on this important matter. You can take these thoughts and use them, or leave them to another reader. We realize there are many practical ways to start a church and no one has the only way, but this is the model we have seen from a diligent study of Baptist history. We do hope that what you read will cause you to pray about your part in fulfilling this oft neglected aspect of the Great Commission.

We have personally put this model into action and have seen the fruit it produces. We will now look briefly at the advantages of this scriptural method and demonstrate how it leads to a multiplying effect of ministry.

Chapter 3
A Superior Model
For the Churches and
the Family of the Church Planter

> "I make bold to say that these Separate Baptists have
> proved to be the most remarkable body of Christians
> America has known."[1]
> —George Washington Paschal

When I graduated from Bible college I could hardly wait to
unleash my dynamic ministry on the world. I was going to build
the biggest church in the universe, complete with grand tiered
parking lots, electric walkways and air conditioned shuttle services.
My church was going to dwarf that of every legend in the history of
the New Testament churches.

That was a shameful and sinful motivation. God knew it. As time
went by, I began to know it.

About 10 years into the ministry, in the dim light of an early
morning, I sat up in bed and realized I probably was never going to
have 10,000 in Sunday school. It was a sad day for me, but it was
also a liberating day. From that point in my life I began to earnestly
ask God what HE wanted me to do with my life. In short, I began
to find the will of God and do it.

Not long after that epiphany, I was led of God to research revival
history in my hometown of St. Louis, Missouri. I was so fascinated
with the early pioneers and how they planted their churches. I
wanted to know just how they did it. I was surprised that in the
beginning days of the town of St. Louis, it was illegal to minister if
you were not a Roman Catholic. Our Baptist forefathers actually
preached while standing in the Mississippi River to avoid
incarceration.

Those early pioneers carved out churches. It was very slow at the
outset, but through patient labor and a simple plan, those early

---

1 George Washington Paschal, *History of North Carolina Baptists vol. 1*
(Raleigh: Edwards & Broughton Co., 1930), P. 240.

churches became mighty forces for good in the community. God spoke very clearly to me through this study about the value of planting churches.

In 1997, after much prayer, we launched into this effort in earnest by assisting in our first church planting effort.

Not long after, I attended a Baptist history tour. During that tour, I felt led of God to write exclusively on the subject of Baptist history. What I discovered validated my burden to plant churches. The release of our book, *America in Crimson Red* helped galvanize the resolve of our church in the planting of new works. Beginning in 1997, we have been privileged by the grace of God to assist in the planting of five churches. These churches are in the St. Louis, or eastern Missouri area.

In the course of research and writing, it was troubling to see that Baptist heritage had been forsaken. Not only was the stellar testimony of the Baptists ignored or eradicated, their ministry model of preaching the Gospel and gathering churches had been forsaken. It was painfully obvious that the Baptists had a forgotten ministry model. As will be demonstrated, it was the Separate Baptist church planting revival in the South (1755 and beyond) that brought biblical revival and direction to our fledgling country.[2]

We have often said that the study of Baptist history and living the heritage will benefit three areas: It will benefit our knowledge of *theology*, *ministry model*, and *civil government principles*. As for our purpose in this volume, we will concentrate on the *ministry model*. We will find a superior model in the scriptural and historical testimony of the *Separate Baptists*.

To begin with, the scriptural plan of ministry is obvious. Matthew 28:19-20 is the Great Commission:

> "Go ye therefore, and teach all nations, baptizing them in the name of the Father, and of the Son, and of the Holy Ghost: Teaching them to observe all things whatsoever I have commanded you: and, lo, I am with you alway, even unto the end of the world. Amen."—

---

2 For more information see the author's book, *America in Crimson Red*, chapters 7-13.

7

Matthew 28:19-20

We see the obvious outline here, but often we overlook the end product. We are to go, preach, baptize, and teach. This makes the materials available to form a living organization called a *church*. This living body grows, matures, and if it has not been stymied by malnourishment brings forth more churches. This is indicated by this passage:

> "Then had **the churches** rest throughout all Judaea and Galilee and Samaria, and were edified; and walking in the fear of the Lord, and in the comfort of the Holy Ghost, **were multiplied**."—Acts 9:31

Notice that it is the **churches** that are **multiplied**. Go back and read it again. Church planting is a natural progression stemming from obedience to the Great Commission. Consider Psalm 1:1-3:

> "Blessed is the man that walketh not in the counsel of the ungodly, nor standeth in the way of sinners, nor sitteth in the seat of the scornful. But his delight is in the law of the LORD; and in his law doth he meditate day and night. And he shall be like a tree planted by the rivers of water, that bringeth forth his fruit in his season; his leaf also shall not wither; and whatsoever he doeth shall prosper."

Since this is a practical handbook, and not a theological apology, we will keep the concept of church planting simple. If the fruit of a Christian is another Christian, then it follows that the fruit of a church is another church. This should be the natural progression of every church.

Churches send missionary evangelists such as Paul and Barnabas or Paul and Silas. But let us take it a step further. At times Paul assumed the office of a pastor. He launched new works while in that office. He encouraged Timothy to do the same. He encouraged Titus to do the same. **Established pastors ought to initiate new works**. Existing churches ought to plant churches in their Judea as illustrated by Titus and his actions on the island of Crete.

8

What we want our reader to see immediately is the model, a model used not only in the first century, but throughout all ages of Baptist ancestry.

The *baptized believers*, identified by their rejection of infant christening and the control of the church-state establishment, survived by multiplying their churches. This was accomplished underground. This was the method of such groups as the Donatists, Paulicians, Waldensians, and other so-called heretical groups throughout the ages.

The promise of Ephesians 3:21: "Unto him be glory in the church by Christ Jesus **throughout all ages**, world without end. Amen," means that somehow the churches of Jesus Christ would survive. The only way they could have survived would have been through reproduction. We mean a multiplication not just of converts, but of churches.

The most productive Christians in American history are also the direct progenitors of the independent Baptists—the Separate Baptists. These hearty and courageous people practiced the model of Titus. They ministered the words of God during the late 18th and early 19th centuries. The leader of the revival, humanly speaking, was Shubal Stearns, an obscure but singularly blessed man. Other men followed Stearns including: Samuel Harriss, John Taylor, Daniel Marshall, Tidence Lane, and Jeremiah Vardemann. All of these men were pastors or evangelists who planted churches at an astonishing rate.

If you knew of a man that God used to bring about the planting of 1,000 churches, would you want to learn from him? Would you want to learn the ministry model of the men he trained? The model of the Separate Baptists is both superior and more scriptural than most of what is presented as church models at this present hour.

The Separate Baptists had no money. Their churches were never very big. They had no backing from the established order. They had no help from millionaires. They were falsely accused of being uneducated, rowdy and out of order. They never protected their momentum. They never had their picture or sermons printed in a famous publication. In fact, they never had their portraits done at all. Yet they were responsible for the transformation of the South,

9

and with that, the transformation of the entire nation. The late David L. Cummins, the most highly respected Baptist historian of our day wrote:

> "As a result of the evangelism and enthusiasm of the Separate Baptists, the Gospel saturated North and South Carolina, Virginia, Georgia, Tennessee and Kentucky. George Washington Paschal opined: 'I make bold to say that these Separate Baptists have proved to be the most remarkable body of Christians America has known.'
>
> As we witness our nation in such spiritual disarray, we can but thrill and cry out to our sovereign God, 'Lord, do it again.' Surely the Lord of Glory blessed the efforts of these indefatigable evangelists with His presence and power. Morgan Edwards, early Baptist researcher and historian, wrote of the Separate Baptists in these words: 'I believe a preternatural and invisible hand works in the assemblies of the Separate-Baptists bearing down the human mind, as was the case in the primitive churches.'[3]

I am an independent Baptist. I have examined the history of our own churches. The evidence shows that the independent Baptists of today have been instructed to copy a model for church that is not their own. We have a heritage on how to do church, but we are not following it.

It is evident that we independent Baptists have given umbrage to the history of Fundamentalism and not the historic Baptists. While this issue is not the intent or scope of this book, it is strange that we have lauded the champions of Protestantism while ignoring our own history. Does it matter? Is this about sour grapes? No, not at all.

This is about our unique model of doing church. This is about a model that led to the greatest revival in the history of America. By embracing Fundamentalist history instead of our own unique heritage, we have stumbled in the dark, not quite knowing what to do with our present predicament. We find ourselves trying to repeat the exploits of ecumenical styled revivalists, rather than repeat the simple New Testament model of multiplying our churches.

---

3 http://www.21tnt.com/archive_for_articles/separatebbb.htm

The multiplying model is superior both historically and scripturally. And when it is used it is also less taxing on the family of the church planter.

We have experienced the pressures of planting a new church. It is especially difficult for the wife of the church planter. Many times the wife is tending to babies during the services or she may be playing the piano. She may do most of the paperwork. When the model in this book is used, the church planter and his family have an existing church home. They work out of the sowing church. There is fellowship. The church planter and his wife have help. They are not going to conduct three or four services a week in the beginning using this model. They will have some real support. This model is superior for the home of the church planter.

The country is in trouble. By being spellbound with an unreasonable affection to mega-church models, we have been left impotent. What we could receive from our Baptist forefathers—a far superior model—has been lying dormant on the pages of neglected history.

The Separate Baptists knew nothing about the empire-styled super church. They had no interest in keeping their movement going. Yet they planted over 1,000 churches in one generation and led the greatest revival in American history. Let us return to their biblical model before it is eternally too late.

Chapter 4
What is God Trying to Tell Us?

> "But ye shall receive power, after that the Holy Ghost is
> come upon you: and ye shall be witnesses unto me both
> in Jerusalem, and in all Judaea, and Samaria, and unto
> the uttermost part of the earth."—Acts 1:8

Since 2004 we have been beating the drum for church planting among the distracted independent Baptists. We are not alone in telling and practicing this message. Numbers of individual pastors have caught the vision of their forefathers and rekindled the fires of winning souls in Judaea and gathering them into local New Testament churches.

In the early part of 2007, I was invited to attend a planning session of Pastors School at First Baptist Church, Hammond, Indiana. I am a 1983 graduate of Hyles-Anderson College, and since my alma-mater has had little or nothing to do with our writings, researches, findings, etc., I felt compelled to make the visit in hopes of having some opportunity for influence.

I was to sit with a panel of roughly a dozen men and discuss the history of the Baptists in America and their methods. The action of the committee was a revelation to me.

The meeting began with an examination of a dated list of the 100 largest churches in America. The panel was shown the list from the year 1972. Next we were shown the list of the 100 largest churches from the current year.

The comparison was striking. In 1972, most of the largest 100 churches in America were independent Baptist churches. However, in the current listing, there were just handfuls from the independent Baptist persuasion.

Therefore a question was posed: What did it mean? How did this happen? How did the independent Baptists suffer such a fall? A discussion by the panel ensued.

Most of the men concluded that something had gone awry with the independent Baptists. It was suggested that we must be side-tracked, that somehow we had become misguided. Various causes

12

for our misdirection were given. Could it be our methods? Could it be our doctrine? It was suggested that perhaps our fight for the King James Bible somehow distracted us. Another theory was the division among the various personalities within the independent ranks had choked our growth.

How could the Charismatics, Pentecostals, and the Southern Baptists have passed the independents in attendance and power? Around the conference table men gave their opinions. The discussion came to me. I was asked from a historical perspective, what could be wrong?

I suggested that there might not be anything wrong with our doctrine or our stand on the Bible. Perhaps if a church took a strong stand for God's word, it may not be the biggest. Perhaps we were concerned about men reaching a certain level that their abilities and their God would not allow them to reach. I suggested that the problem was really ministry model. In the past God used a group of churches in the Baptist ranks to bring revival. These were the Separate Baptists, and none of their churches ever reached a magic number of 1,000 in attendance.

The committee wanted some figures on the size of the churches among the Separate Baptists. I told them that as near as we could ascertain, the largest church among them was Shubal Stearns' Sandy Creek Baptist Church with just over 600 members. They also wanted some figures on the average size of the churches among the Separate Baptists. I told them that as near as we could ascertain, the average attendance was around 75. They seemed disappointed with these numbers.

I pressed the point that perhaps if a pastor takes the proper stand, he may not be the biggest or the most popular, but he could be a part of the solution. He could help save the country. I further suggested that if the preachers were taught they should achieve some certain number in attendance, the effect would only be *discouragement*. It may not be the size of the church that mattered. I suggested that it might be that God is trying to tell us something else. He may be telling us to multiply our effort by planting churches as our Baptist heritage vividly illustrates.

I do not believe that our problem is a lack of super-churches, nor do I believe our problem stems from an unbalanced view of issues. I contend and have contended since the publishing of *America in Crimson Red* in 2004, that our problem is **ministry model**. We have rejected the scriptural model of our Separate Baptist forefathers. We are not planting churches from our existing churches. Our pastors are not leading out. I suggested to the committee, that although the churches of the Separate Baptist movement did not achieve mega-size, they were used of God to save the country and transform the South into a republic-loving, Bible-believing bastion of liberty.

1,000 church plants in 25 years among the Separate Baptists is hard to ignore. An estimated 5,000 churches sprang in the next generation. Nearly all of the churches of the South, including the rise of the independent Baptists came from this revival. It is to this ministry model, the model of the Separate Baptists, we ought to repair.

Chapter 5
Has God Ever Saved America?

> "We must either deny all influence to the preaching of democratic and individualistic ideas in religion, or we must admit that the preaching of Stearns and his fellow laborers quickened the spirit of democracy among their hearers."—George Washington Paschal

Has God ever saved America? If He has, how did it happen?

In his book, *The Transformation of Virginia*, Rhys Isaac described the conversion of James Ireland. Ireland was of Scot descent, a wild fiddler and worldling who was living out his rebellion on the Virginia frontier. When salvation came to James Ireland, the entire community took note and feared. It changed things. This kind of thing happened all over the colony of Virginia. Revival broke out among the Virginians several times from 1764 to 1788. John Leland, the revivalist pastor, church planter, and American statesman described it:

"From the year 1764, [the Baptists] prevailed so much, that, in the year following, they formed an Association, called, the Ketocton Regular Baptist Association. From 1764 to 1774, the Baptists spread over the greatest part of the state that was peopled. Several ministers, of that order came from Pennsylvania and the Jerseys, and settled in the northern parts of the state, and others were raised up in the southern parts, who traveled about, and preached like the old Baptist, John, 'repent, for the kingdom of Heaven is at hand, and great numbers of the people went out unto them, and were baptized, confessing their sins.'

Many of the young converts caught the spirit of their teachers, and zealously engaged in the work."[4]

Isaac may have inadvertently given the reason for the transformation of Virginia, but Leland positively identified it. It was the revival produced by the preaching and church planting

---

4 Leland, Elder John. *The Writings of Elder John Leland, Including Some Events in his Life.* New York, NY: G. W. Wood, 1845. P.104-105.4

exploits of the Separate Baptists.

A strong case could be made that God saved the country from tyranny and sin in the beginning stages of her forming. If this is so, then it should stir careful examination in the hope that it might happen again.

The revival of the Separate Baptists had its beginning in 1755, when Shubal Stearns and his associate, Daniel Marshall came to the central west settlements of North Carolina.

Stearns was from New England and was converted in the Great Awakening. After studying the issue, he was baptized by immersion by Wait Palmer, leaving Congregationalism.

There was formidable opposition to the preacher in North Carolina. The Church of England was the established church and gave no liberty to dissenters. Stearns began immersing his converts in Sandy Creek. Some of the men of the backcountry and piedmont areas of North Carolina, with their Church of England background, began to swear oaths to never become a Baptist.[5]

Yet one pioneer, Tidence Lane, had a desire to hear the preacher. Even with the criticisms of Stearns' loud voice and gestures, Lane believed seeing Mr. Stearns might be entertaining. Lane rode east from the Yadkin River to the crossroads at Sandy Creek. He later testified:

"When the fame of Mr. Stearns' preaching had reached the Yadkin, I felt a curiosity to go and hear him. Upon my arrival I saw a venerable old man sitting under a peach-tree with a book in his hand and the people gathering about him. He fixed his eyes upon me immediately, which made me feel in such a manner as I have never felt before. I turned to quit the place but could not proceed far. I walked about, sometimes catching his eyes as I walked. My uneasiness increased and it became intolerable. I went up to him thinking that a salutation and shaking hands would relieve me: but it happened otherwise. I began to think that he had an evil eye and ought to be shunned; but shunning him I could no more effect than a bird can shun a rattlesnake when it fixes its eyes upon it. When he began to preach my

---

5 James Ireland, *The Life of the Rev. James Ireland*, (Winchester: J. Foster, 1819), P. 72.

perturbations increased so that nature could no longer support them and I sunk to the ground."[6]

Morgan Edwards described the preaching and ministry of Shubal Stearns:

"His voice was musical and strong, which he managed in such a manner as to make soft impressions on the heart, and fetch tears in the eyes in a mechanical way; and anon, to shake the very nerves and throw the animal system into tumults and perturbations."[7]

The preachers who surrendered to the call of God under the ministry of Shubal Stearns took on similar characteristics, not just in preaching style, but in character.

His associate, Daniel Marshall, birthed churches in North Carolina, Virginia, South Carolina and Georgia.

James Read and eventually John Leland saw revival in Virginia. William and Joseph Murphy were converted under Stearns. Their most notable convert was Samuel Harriss.

Harriss began preaching throughout Virginia and a list of notable converts under his ministry included John Weatherford, Anderson Moffett, and Lewis and Elijah Craig. Harriss was compared to George Whitefield. Robert Semple tells us that when exhorting at great meetings, Harriss "poured forth streams of celestial lightning from his eyes, which, whithersoever he turned his face, would strike down hundreds at once."[8]

Allen Wyley led Harriss to Culpeper where he preached in his home. The first meeting went well, but the next day an angry crowd met them with whips. A group of angry men, set against the evangelist said, "You shall not preach here."

A Virginia convert, Jeremiah Minor, replied, "But we shall."

The Baptists with Harriss, a converted Virginia colonel now as their spiritual leader, saw no need to desist and a riot broke out. Harriss did preach there. In 40 years of ministry in the state of

---

6 Edwards, *Materials Toward a History of the Baptists of North Carolina*, 387.
7 *Ibid.*
8 *Ibid.*, 380.

Virginia, Samuel Harriss, under God, brought into existence an incomprehensible 60 churches. When we say 60 churches we mean Harriss preached, pastored, baptized, established and installed or ordained pastors in each of those places.

To encourage one another, the preachers among the Separate Baptists met once a year. This meeting produced the third Baptist Association in American history, The Sandy Creek Baptist Association (1758), but they hardly resembled the typical modern Baptist association. The associational meeting was purely for encouragement, training and the planting of new churches.

Since the preachers came from great distances, it became necessary to camp at Sandy Creek. Thus began America's historic camp meetings, an event that defined the American frontier. The roots of southern religion, the form and fashion of revival preaching and even the culture of the South, was germinated at the Sandy Creek camp meeting and exported from there throughout the South.

Robert Semple wrote:

"Thro' these meetings, the gospel was carried into many new places, where the fame of the Baptists had previously spread; for great crowds attending from distant parts, mostly though curiosity, many became enamoured with these extraordinary people, and petitioned the association to send preachers into their neighborhoods. These petitions were readily granted, and the preachers as readily complied with the appointments."[9]

The results of Stearns' ministry:
17 preachers birthed 34 churches
34 churches birthed 128 churches
128 churches birthed 1,000
1,000 birthed 5,000 estimated

The Separate Baptists:
1. **Trained their own men**
2. **Raised no money**

---

9 Robert Baylor Semple, *The Rise and Progress of the Baptists in Virginia* (Richmond, By the Author, 1810), P. 6.

3. Kept the ordinances
4. Had evangelists who did the work, pastors that led as evangelists and evangelists that pastored
5. Planted churches from existing churches using scriptural means

Chapter 6
A Dying Model vs. a Multiplying Model

> "Then had the churches rest throughout all Judaea and
> Galilee and Samaria, and were edified; and walking in
> the fear of the Lord, and in the comfort of the Holy
> Ghost, were multiplied."—Acts 9:31

The ministry model of the Fundamentalist movement has been super-church or empire-church. The problem with this model is that it is neither a Biblical nor a historic Baptist model. In addition, it is practically uncopyable. There may be a few pastors that can produce congregations in the 900 to 10,000 range, but not many.

The New Testament records a very large church at Jerusalem, and another large church at Antioch. However, the vast majority of the churches were not mega-sized, as it remains to this day. The scriptural example of multiplying churches is the prominent model. The embodiment of this model is found in the Separate Baptists of America. Thus as we have stated, it is a vastly superior model. It is practical, copyable and much more effective in meeting the spiritual needs of a community and therefore of the entire country. How do we know this? It is a scriptural reality and a measurable fact.

I will leave the ecumenical Fundamentalists to chase down the church model of the Protestant evangelists (if they can find it) while we rediscover the multiplying ministry model of the Separate Baptists.

Lately, a group of concerned preachers have been reconnecting with their own history. The so-called leadership of the independent Baptists, identified according to their conferences, colleges, and universities, have made no attempt to analyze the fruitful ministry model of the Separate Baptists. This attitude makes the model unavailable for young servants. What our students have been taught is knowledge of Billy Sunday, Gypsy Smith, D. L. Moody, John Calvin, Martin Luther, Zwingli, etc. Hardly any of the men that are held in esteem as leaders to our children were Baptist, and none of them held dear the ordinances of the local church. Therefore, none of them have the correct ministry model.

The tendency is to hold before young servants a heroic empire-style ministry. But that model is a dying model.

The aforementioned committee in Chapter 2 was perplexed at the decline of the largest churches among the independent Baptists, but they should not have been. All churches rise and fall. If they are empire in their model they will rise and fall and die *absolutely*. What I mean is they will die leaving no sprouting churches behind. A church that is not reproducing itself is in a process of dying *absolutely*.

Empire church vs. Church planting church

What do we mean by empire church? What we mean is that model of church ministry which emphasizes the buildup of a single local church. It is a narrow vision of building the local church exclusively, usually for the purpose of drawing together a super church or mega-church. It is no secret that the magic number for mega-church is 1,000.

Let us be honest. Any preacher would love to reach 1,000 people. 1,000 is better for Heaven than 100, but great discernment is needed here. If this is the sole goal of the local church, it is doomed to die *absolutely* one day. Why should your church die ***absolutely***?

Your church will one day be extinct. This is not difficult to prove, as there are many instances of this throughout the centuries. Not one church that the Apostle Paul planted exists today. The churches of the biggest names in Fundamentalism have died or are in the process of dying. When they die, if they have not been in the business of planting churches, then their ministry dies with them.

The model of empire church is an absolute dying model regardless of how super-sized the church becomes, ***unless*** that church reproduces itself in the planting of new churches. I would rather help plant ten churches from our church than have 1,000 in membership. Why? Because the fidelity of those ten churches will last longer than the fidelity of the church that assisted in their planting.

In the early 20th century, the idea of empire church emerged. Organizations were begun under the influence of great leaders or powerful preachers. Moody Church began in the wake of D. L. Moody. Chicago Gospel Center began under the auspices of Paul Rader. The Cadle Tabernacle began under the ministry of Howard Cadle. I am not criticizing these men or their sincerity. I am saying these organizations were not Baptist churches. They were citadels of Fundamentalism and they have died or are going to die *absolutely*. There were numbers of church-like organizations formed in the wake of these men, but they did not obey the Great Commission. They disregarded or corrupted the ordinances of baptism and the Lord's Supper and they disregarded church planting. We could illustrate it in this fashion:

 The empire church springs up with leadership.

 It also goes down with that leadership.

And dies *absolutely*.

 The church planting church springs up also with leadership:

 It also goes down with that leadership.

22

And dies. Yet it lives on in the churches it planted.

If the Apostle Paul had had the mind-set of the average independent Baptist pastor today, the churches of Jesus Christ would have ceased to exist sometime in the second century. Church planting as a multiplying ministry can be seen from the chart of the Separate Baptist churches, listed next, which were planted from Sandy Creek:

These churches were begun in **N. C.**
1- Sandy Creek: 1755, Shubal Stearns
2- Abbot's Creek: 1756, Daniel Marshall
3- Grassy Creek : 1756, James Reed
4- Deep River: 1757, Joseph Murphy, Phillip Mulkey
5- New River: 1758, Ezekiel Hunter
6- Little River: 1759, Joseph Murphy
8-Black River: 1760, John Newton
10- Trent: 1761, James McDaniel
11- Southwest: 1762, Charles Markland
12-Haw River: 1764, Elnathan Davis
Shallow Ford: 1768, Joseph Murphy
Lockwood's Folly: 1772 Nathaniel Powell, James Turner, Ezekial Hunter

> Little River grew to 500 members in 3 years. It had four church plants in ten years:
> Little River 2, Rocky Rvr, Jones Crk, Mountain Crk.

> Haw River from 1765 to 1772 grew to five branches:
> Deep River 2, Rocky River 2, Tick Creek, Collins Mount, Caraway Creek.

These churches were begun in **S. CAROLINA**
9-Fairforest: 1760, Philip Mulkey
Congaree: 1766, Joseph Rees
Stephens Creek: 1766, Daniel Marshall

These churches were begun in **VIRGINIA**
7- Dan River: 1759, Dutton Lane
Upper Spottsylvania Church: 1767, Lewis Craig
Staughton River: 1768, William Murphy
Lower Spottsylvania: 1769, John Waller, Jeremiah Walker
Fall Creek: 1769, Samuel Harris
Goochland: 1771, William Webber

From this initial revival at least 5,000 churches had their rise.

Death is coming to your church one day. You ought to pray, plan and work so that it will not die ***absolutely***.

Chapter 7
Pastor Initiated Church Planting

> "But watch thou in all things, endure afflictions, do the
> work of an evangelist, make full proof of thy
> ministry."—2 Timothy 4:5

> "For this cause left I thee in Crete, that thou shouldest
> set in order the things that are wanting, and ordain
> elders in every city, as I had appointed thee"—Titus 1:5

Let us identify the ministries involved in Titus 1:5. There are
three New Testament ministries at work.

1. Apostle—literally "one sent out" this is Paul. This office
ended with the ministry of Paul. These men were sent directly
from the Lord Jesus during the beginning stages of the early New
Testament churches.

**2. Evangelist—literally "one who cries the good news" this is
Titus in Titus 1:5.** Evangelists are those called of God to preach
the Gospel and gather converts into churches. This means existing
churches or new churches.

3. Elder or Pastor—a God-called ordained leader, a pastor. In
Titus 1:5, the elders mentioned are in the office of **pastor**—the
God-called leadership of a New Testament church.

So then we find:

**Paul (an apostle doing the work of an evangelist) left Titus
(an evangelist who became a pastor) on the island of Crete to
ordain elders (pastors) in every city (where the new churches
were planted).**

In the beginning stages of this model, the established pastor is
the pastor of the new work. In fact, the new work truly is a ministry
of the established *sowing church*. The established pastor will be the
pastor until the right time and the right man is found.

How may this be accomplished? Historically, many of the
Separate Baptists pastored multiple churches. They preached
many, many times each week and were tireless workers. Christmas
Evans did this ministry in Wales. He pastored five churches at the

same time!

At Sandy Creek, their church plants were considered "arms" or "branches" with an "exhorter" who led them until an ordained preacher would come among them and be appointed or elected their pastor.

We have found that an evangelist and an established pastor work well together in the Separate Baptist model. Preaching the Gospel, seeing souls saved and gathering them into local churches is what evangelists *do*.

What is truly needed is for evangelists to be supported. Their support should be enough so that they may invest a larger amount of time in church planting efforts. Support would allow them many weeks or even months in the same place partnering with an established pastor, or a church planter, or both.

Titus, who is our established pastor in the scriptural model, ordains the elders that he himself trained. Ordaining was clearly the work of a pastor, and in this particular case the responsibility of Titus. In our day, the man that comes to take a new and sprouting church may come from the sowing church; or he may come from a distant place; but he ought to be ordained. Until he is, he may be looked upon as an exhorter. The role of the established pastor in our model when he initiates a church plant is vital: Like Titus he is looking for a man to become the elder or pastor of the new church.

There is definitely some overlap in the duties of these ministries in church planting. We believe that Titus was first an evangelist who became a pastor and continued on the work of an evangelist. Titus 1:5 says, "For this cause left I thee in Crete, that thou shouldest:
1. Set in order the things that are wanting, and
2. Ordain elders in every city, as I had appointed thee."

Let us think for a moment about the meaning of the term *missionary*. When a missionary is sent out to a foreign land, we expect that he will preach the Gospel and gather converts into local churches. We may refer to this as mission work, but it is really the work of an evangelist. We would not regard as legitimate the work of a missionary who does not preach the Gospel and gather converts into local churches. The missionary is really an evangelist.

When the subject of home missions or church planting is discussed, there is little understanding of the role of an established pastor in this work. When we think of church-planting we usually think of a very young man, called by God to a needy place, going into a dark tunnel aided only by prayer and a sum of money thrown at him.

Perhaps we should be thinking of Titus instead, who was left on the island of Crete, where he and his church assisted in the planting of a number of churches.

The model of the Separate Baptists of America was done after the manner of Titus. The pastors of the Separate Baptist churches did the work of evangelists, with the Apostle Paul and Titus as their biblical examples and Shubal Stearns and Daniel Marshall as their contemporary examples. It was not complicated. It was just plain obedience to the example of the word of God.

Why not follow this example? Our church has followed this model or some modification of it since 1999 and the success rate has been wonderful.

Again we say, "Established pastors ought to initiate church planting."

A suggestive note is needed here.

The established pastor who is led to launch out to start a church and the church planter who is led to plant a church need to find each other. A true evangelist could come to help them both. We support this kind of plan. With prayer and communication, these men of God ought to find one another. Our web site, multiplyingmodel.com is designed to do just that. I am talking about joining the established pastor, the church planter and an evangelist together. The evangelist would have to understand the model to help bring a church to fruition.

In order for this to happen, there must be re-education on the New Testament example of Titus and a new emphasis on the ministry of the evangelist.

In the case of a distant call, where there is no established pastor, should we not send an evangelist to help that church planter in his effort?

27

May God give us more pastors that are evangelists. There are very few of these men around today, but their numbers are beginning to grow.

Chapter 8
Modifications on the Multiplying Model

No two church plants are the same and the assistance in each case will differ as well. Here are some modifications on the model:

1. The established pastor pastors the new work for an extended period of time. If the new church is chartered, constituted or publically formed right away, he may pastor two churches at one time, waiting for the right man to take the new work.

2. The established pastor and church lay the ground work for the new church by securing property, distributing literature, or doing the work of the sowing stage (see Chapter 13).

3. An established pastor and his church may simply assist a church planter sent by another church. They may come to sit as a church, provide support, provide housing, provide groceries, provide a place to meet, or any combination. In this case, an established pastor and his church may simply help provide a launching place.

4. Some church plants start off a little more advanced and there may be a number of families ready. However, even in this case, that church planter is sent out by an established church.

Obviously, while the established pastor is conducting the services of the new work, he is in his office as pastor. When the church planter arrives on the scene with the intent to become the pastor, the church planter is an exhorter, that is, he is an evangelist doing the work of a pastor until the church is chartered or publically formed and he is installed or called.

Chapter 9
The Need is Also the Solution:
Chief Cities

> "And from thence to Philippi, which is the chief city of
> that part of Macedonia, and a colony: and we were in
> that city abiding certain days."—Acts 16:12

> "To preach the gospel in the regions beyond you, and
> not to boast in another man's line of things made ready
> to our hand."—2 Corinthians 10:16

Have you thought about the chief cities of America? Someone
needs to consider this. The overwhelming need in America is in the
tangled web of sin and pain that is her chief cities.

To obey the great commission, win the lost, disciple converts,
and truly affect the culture, the Biblical model of church planting is
far superior to any Evangelical or Fundamentalist empire building
model.

American cities are sick with sin and in need of repentance. The
need is Jesus Christ and we know who He is. Bible believing
Baptists have abandoned the cities of America, leaving a void. Sin
and false religion is filling that void.

For at least 60 years, the independent Baptists have fallen
behind. We have labored for an ideal that is impractical to help
small towns, counties or neighborhoods of the inner city.

In the early 20th century, America passed from its gilded age into
the modern era. With this, the decline of the American city began.
Scores of major cities lost population and businesses from inside
the city limits. Churches that were once great proponents of the
Gospel began to deteriorate and most migrated out of the cities.
This was universal in its scope. From Boston to San Francisco, the
inner city churches of bye-gone days moved to suburban areas.
This suburban migration left a vacuum never remedied.

Only two things can happen if the Gospel is removed from a city.
Either that city will become steeped in sin, or it will become
engulfed in false doctrine.

Let us take Los Angeles for example. In 2010, within the city

30

limits of L.A. there are 3.8 millions of people. Among this population, there are 63 Mormon congregations (perhaps as many as 600 in the surrounding counties), 40 Jehovah's Witness Kingdom Halls (at least 215 in the surrounding area), 48 Muslim mosques or centers and a sum total of 4 independent Baptist churches within the city limits.

These shocking figures are repeated in nearly every major American city.

Here are some statistics from simply perusing the phone book. These do not include the surrounding areas, just within the city limits. Although not exact, the numbers are very close and show the stark reality of an unanswered need.

New York City Limits
Population: 8.2 million
Mormon Congregations: 23
Jehovah's Witness Kingdom Halls: 14
Muslim Mosques or centers: 10
Independent Baptist Churches: 5

San Francisco City Limits
Population: 765,000
Mormon Congregations: 12
Jehovah's Witness Kingdom Halls: 4
Muslim Mosques or centers: 2
Independent Baptist Churches: 4

Cleveland City Limits
Population: 450,000
Mormon Congregations: 10
Jehovah's Witness Kingdom Halls: 16
Muslim Mosques or centers: 4
Independent Baptist Churches: 9

San Jose City Limits
Population: 1 million
Mormon Congregations: 14

Jehovah's Witness Kingdom Halls: 4
Muslim Mosques or centers: 7
Independent Baptist Churches: 2

Philadelphia City Limits
Population: 1.4 million
Mormon Congregations: 10
Jehovah's Witness Kingdom Halls: 25
Muslim Mosques or centers: 5
Independent Baptist Churches: 12

Detroit City Limits
Population: 900,000
Mormon Congregations: 46
Jehovah's Witness Kingdom Halls: 22
Muslim Mosques or centers: 100
Independent Baptist Churches: 5

Consider Boston, Chicago, Atlanta, Miami, Richmond, DC, Philly, NYC, Cleveland, Cincinnati, Detroit, Charlotte, Charleston, St. Louis, Kansas City, Memphis, Minneapolis, Tulsa, Dallas, Houston, San Fran, LA, Seattle, Portland, San Diego, Milwaukee, Madison, Salt Lake City, New Orleans, Denver, Tampa, Honolulu, Las Vegas, etc. all of these cities are in a similar situation.

A deficient plan for the major cities was given to independent Baptists in the 70's, 80's and 90's. I recall a man coming to the St. Louis, Missouri area to start a church. I was a Bible college student at the time. He attended a well known Baptist college. Even though I was away from St. Louis most of the time, I tried to be a help to this man whenever I was home. As a young preacher, I was very interested in the planting of churches, especially in my home town. This man really struggled. He really did not have a "sowing church" from which the new church could spring.

He was taught that in order to reach a large metro area, you must find a good suburb and plant a great work. Then the people of the city would come to you. This is the "suburban empire church" model.

But I doubted the validity of this model even as a college boy. Because I was from the city, I knew quite well that only rarely do city people drive to the suburbs for anything. Large numbers do not even own cars. The idea of suburban empire church reaching over distances does not work. It never reached the cities and it never will. The church planter I have described was left to fend for himself, had no sowing church and failed to plant a church.

So what must we do? In order to solve the monumental problem of America's cities, we need to obey the Great Commission and carry it out to its logical conclusion: Win souls in the cities and gather those converted into churches. Believe me, the Mormons have a plan and have been carrying it out. The Jehovah's Witnesses have a plan and have been carrying it out. Frighteningly, the Muslims have a plan and are faithfully executing it.

Is there any hope for our great American urban areas? We know it is the Gospel of Jesus Christ and the planting of churches. This is the only hope of the hour.

Our plan should be simple. The churches that ring the outskirts of our American urban areas ought to be assisting in the planting of churches within the city limits. If the pastors of the suburban churches would step outside the box and view themselves as evangelists, a real revival could ensue. We do not need money-making plans for this; we need only to copy the example of the Separate Baptist revival with its strong pastoral leadership, and their practice of sitting as a church.

On the south side of St. Louis, there is a recent church plant, the Gateway Baptist Church. This sprouting church is pastored by Daniel McCrillis and has seen many souls come to Christ. They have been effective in helping others with addictions, and by the grace of God have put some families back together. This is in the inner city woefully in need of an aggressive Gospel witness. When a liquor store across the street from the church applied for a new license, the young church succeeded in shutting that harmful entity down. Gateway is a neighborhood church. They are there where the people need them. We compared the crime rates for the Patch neighborhood in the city of St. Louis, Missouri. Patch is the location of Gateway Baptist Church. St. Louis has had one of the highest crime rates of any major city in America. The chart displays the crime rate for the year the Gateway Baptist Church was begun (2005-2006), and then after a period of three years (2008). The decrease in crime for the neighborhood is a significant 33%. While we know other factors are certainly involved, the testimony of Bro. McCrillis may shed some light on the decrease:

ST. LOUIS METROPOLITAN POLICE DEPARTMENT CRIME SUMMARY BY NEIGHBORHOOD 2005

NEIGHBORHOOD	TOTAL MURDER	TOTAL RAPE	ROBBERY TOTAL	ROBBERY ARMED	AGG. ASSAULT TOTAL	AGG. ASSAULT W/GUN	SUB-TOTAL PERSON	TOTAL BURGLARY	TOTAL LARCENY	AUTO THEFT	TOTAL ARSON	SUB-TOTAL PROPERTY	TOTAL INDEX CRIME
Patch	1	4	11	6	48	13	64	73	233	69	10	385	449

CRIME SUMMARY BY NEIGHBORHOOD 2008

NEIGHBORHOOD	TOTAL MURDER	TOTAL RAPE	ROBBERY TOTAL	ROBBERY ARMED	AGG. ASSAULT TOTAL	AGG. ASSAULT W/GUN	SUB-TOTAL PERSON	TOTAL BURGLARY	TOTAL LARCENY	AUTO THEFT	TOTAL ARSON	SUB-TOTAL PROPERTY	TOTAL INDEX CRIME
Patch	0	3	13	7	44	10	60	70	123	43	4	240	300

"We've seen probably three or four hundred people saved in the three years we've been here. We've seen75-100 adults baptized. Over time you have that slow change. The prostitutes are not here anymore. The place across the street does not sell open liquor bottles anymore. The community is a much better place. People don't mind living here now."

Up to now, there is no alarm sounding from the leadership of the distracted independent Baptist movement for the unbelievable need of our American cities. There has been no articulation of either the problem or a plan to redeem our cities from sudden and sure destruction. This woeful need is to our knowledge, never mentioned in any major conference, pastor's convention, or college. Concerning the needs of America's chief cities, the independent Baptists have been all but silent.

34

Chapter 10
The Most Important Dynamic of the Multiplying Model:
Sitting as a Church

> "With Onesimus, a faithful and beloved brother, **who is one of you**. They shall make known unto you all things which are done here."—Col. 4:9

> "Epaphras, **who is one of you**, a servant of Christ, saluteth you."—Col. 4:12

Sitting as a church is the single most important dynamic to the Separate Baptist model. The Sandy Creek Baptist Church, under the leadership of Shubal Stearns used the concept of sitting as a church to great advantage. According to Robert Devin, the author of *the History of the Grassy Creek Baptist Church*, Sandy Creek would birth a church in this manner: Members would journey to a needy area and *sit as a church* under the preaching of a man of God.[10] They would *sit** to encourage the work; they would work to bring people to the services and they would win converts. When the proper time would come, a preacher would be ordained to pastor the new church. Then they would move on. This work went on continuously with several missions occurring simultaneously.[11]

Sitting as a church means simply: The members of an established church visit the services of a sprouting church and lend physical, mental and especially spiritual strength to the sprouting church.

We believe this is the ministry of Onesimus and Epaphras found in the book of Colossians. They were at a mission work to help encourage and teach those in the new work. They did not stay at the new work, they came home, but their time was valuable. Very simple, but this is a powerful tool and makes a difference. It is

---

10 Robert I. Devin, *A History of the Grassy Creek Baptist Church* (Raleigh: Edwards, Broughten and Co., 1880), P. 92.

* This would not necessarily be the same *sitters* at the same infant church every week.

11 This is the human explanation for the birthing of 42 churches in 15 years, and the birthing of over 1,000 within 30 years.

scriptural and we have seen the benefits by experience. Pastor Joe Esposito of Pacific Baptist Church of Long Beach, California describes it:

> "Some of our people (sometimes called 'sitters,' sometimes called other names) that is, a handful of families participated in the new church when it started. In this way you can have some greeters; you can have people that are actually singing from the very first service. You can have people that love God in the services. Loving God is contagious. That is what we did. Our people, our church, started a church 18 miles away."

Below you will find a typical sign-up sheet used by our church during a time of sitting as a church. It is a simple sign-up sheet that directs volunteers to gave some time and treasure to a new church plant. Notice those who chose to help signed on the left to sit as a church. Those that volunteered to help financially did so by signing on the right side for what we termed *grocery money*. The amount set for grocery money was roughly $75.00 for a one-time gift. We asked the volunteers to give at least once every six months in the crucial first 2 year period. The grocery money was given directly to the church planter who came to take the sprouting church.

Grace Independent Baptist Church

Bro. Matt Dudley Pastor   314-808-2048
3774 Hess Road, House Springs, MO 63051
at the corner of Hiway 30 and Upper Byrnes Mill

SIT AS A CHURCH	PROVIDE GROCERIES ($75 per week)
SEPTEMBER 4 *Bohnert*	SEPTEMBER 4 *Bohnert*
SEPTEMBER 11 *Stout Malady*	SEPTEMBER 11 *McCannett*
SEPTEMBER 18	SEPTEMBER 18 *Mrs. Dekot*
SEPTEMBER 25 *Rich Dickerson*	SEPTEMBER 25 *RETIERS*
OCTOBER 2 *For Seawoon*	OCTOBER 2 *Don Seawoon*
OCTOBER 9 *(scribble)*	OCTOBER 9 *Rich Dickerson*
OCTOBER 16 *The Hawkins*	OCTOBER 16 *The Hawkins*
OCTOBER 23	OCTOBER 23 *Rich Dickerson*
OCTOBER 30 *Alex v Christina Jerkeona*	OCTOBER 30 *Prossion*

37

Part 2
The Model in Practice

Chapter 11
What Happened

We will now give three testimonies from our own church efforts to assist church plants using the multiplying model.

SOLID ROCK BAPTIST CHURCH

In the beginning days of our first church plant assist, I made a trip to a Bible college and was asked to give a short testimony. I stood in front of the students and told them about the burden of our church to plant churches in the city of St. Louis. It was not my intention to recruit anyone from the student body, but I did ask them to pray and ask the Lord if they should come to St. Louis to plant a church.

A young man, Joe Cassada, approached me after the chapel service and asked me a number of questions about the city of St. Louis. After going home, we communicated by telephone and letter and this was the man whom God sent to the first church plant in which Arnold Baptist Tabernacle assisted.

In the beginning, we provided housing for the Cassadas. They joined our church and helped in our Christian School. We prepared the church to give to the new work and to sit as a church.

Bro. Cassada began in the Affton area of St. Louis in a store front. He worked very hard taking the Gospel door to door. And God blessed him. Eventually the time came for a more permanent place.

We visited a church building in the Rock Hill area of St. Louis. It was a good fit for the infant church. Arnold Baptist Tabernacle secured a loan for the building for $100,000. Solid Rock Baptist Church sent half of the monthly mortgage in the form of love offerings. Eventually they covered the entire note each month. The time came when they purchased the building from us for $90,000. This action puzzled our banker who thought we had taken a loss, but to us it was an investment.

For the first two years, our people gave weekly grocery money and sat as a church. Some visited, some worked nursery, some personally helped Bro. Cassada and his young family. Everybody prayed fervently. We tried to come along side and be a blessing.

Solid Rock Baptist Church chartered as a church and continued to grow. They later sold their original building and purchased another. They continue to reach people for the Lord.

GATEWAY BAPTIST CHURCH

Feeling led of the Spirit to help plant a church on the extreme south side of the city of St. Louis, we launched a Bible study which was held on Sunday afternoons in the living room of one of our members. This church member lived on the extreme south side of St. Louis and was more than willing to open his home to Sunday afternoon services.

There was a couple in our church, Dave and Penny Parshall, who took an interest in helping with this church plant. Bro. Parshall's father is a veteran missionary to Australia and the Parshalls had a desire to serve God in the work of starting a church.

Bro. & Mrs. Parshall helped with visitation and provided special music each week. I preached there in the living room in the afternoon for over a year.

On the surface it appeared that nothing happened there, nothing at all. We preached and visited for over a year and saw a handful saved on visitation, but no one was interested in the new work. But we preached faithfully anyway each week singing and praying and teaching with the windows open in that neighborhood.

An opportunity arose in the summer of 2003. An old store front building which had been converted into a church became available at a very reasonable price. The asking price for the building was $60,000. It included a full basement, street level chapel and a second story apartment. It was in pretty rough condition, but it had great potential.

Our deacons at the time thought it had potential also and boldly said that we should make an offer of $30,000 on the building. To our complete surprise the offer was accepted, and we rolled up our sleeves and got busy fixing up the building. We called it the Broadway Chapel as it was on the corner of Broadway and Davis in south St. Louis.

This book is not about how to renovate buildings, but one note is appropriate here. Most churches have men who are more than capable of fixing a church building and getting it ready to have church services. Let your people be used of God in this area. They will have fruit that remains.

Bro. Parshall held services in this building for nearly three years. We sat as a church, and had regular visitation. Bro. & Mrs. Parshall faithfully knocked doors in the neighborhood during that time. This was a sowing time, a period of sowing that led to the birth of Gateway Baptist Church.

In 2006, I received a telephone call from missionary James Waymire who was the founding pastor of Arnold Baptist Tabernacle. He said that he had met a young man, Daniel McCrillis, who was saved in St. Louis and had a desire to return to the city and plant a church. I soon met with Bro. McCrillis and felt led to assist him in a work at the Broadway Chapel.

In the Fall of 2006, Bro. McCrillis moved into the upstairs apartment, and began to visit in the neighborhood. We began to support him with grocery money and to sit as a church. Bro. McCrillis was soon joined by Jesse Middleton and within two years Gateway Baptist Church was averaging over 75 in attendance. Here is Brother McCrillis' testimony about Gateway Baptist Church:

"One day I went to my Dad's house in St. Louis. He talked about the city of St. Louis. He started talking about the people here. I knew the Lord was dealing with my heart, and I told him that night, 'Lord, if you want me to go to St. Louis and start a church I will do that.' I decided to come down and just visit the area.

When I came here to start the church, my wife and I moved here to the property, and Bro. Beller's church had a couple families that actually came here for a year or two and helped out. A check every month came in the mail from the church. And then some of the people helped every month and still do three years later. They pulled right up alongside of us. They didn't just say 'ok, here you go. You're on your own.'

My wife and I went soul winning. Our first service we had 7 people. We had a $7.00 offering for our first offering. My wife said, 'How are we going to make it on $7.00.' I said, 'We're going to thank the Lord. That's how we're going to do it.'

We didn't go on deputation. We did it without having to go out there on that trail. In three years we're already on our own. I think about a year a half ago, we said, 'Let's run with it, and see what we can do.' I needed to know that God was in this thing.

Right now we average about 50 pretty solid people, adults that attend weekly. When we first came here to St. Louis to start the church, to kind of give you an idea of the area, there were prostitutes out in front; homeless guys would camp out on our front door. There was a lot of riff-raff. It wasn't really a safe place. The store across the street was robbed every 2 or 3 months. Eventually, within weeks we started witnessing and getting the Gospel to these people and being a good testimony to them.

One day a lady and a man were out in front of the building. They were involved in drugs and she would go away for a little while and come back. I knew what was going on. I said to my wife, 'Christa, I'll be back in a minute.'

I went out there and talked to the people, 'Hey, I know what you guys are doing here. I live upstairs, this is a church. I would appreciate it if you would do what you're doing somewhere else.'

And they said 'I'm sorry pastor.' Then I said, 'Let me ask you guys a question, What are you doing this for anyway? You know God loves you very much.' I talked to them for about an hour and that man and that lady were in tears crying asking Jesus to come into their heart and save them.

I lost track of them, but about a year ago, I was over here at Church's Chicken going through the drive through, and that same lady was at the window. She was the manager. She said, 'You don't remember me do you?'

I said, 'No, you're going to have to help me.' She said, 'I was the lady that you talked to one day at the side of your church building with my boyfriend.' I said, 'Oh that's you— unbelievable!' I was so happy for her. She looked totally different.

She said, 'Ever since that day, my life has been different. I go to church in another place, but my whole life has been turned around.'

About a block down the way on the east side of our street there was a really big drug dealer, probably one of the biggest ones in the area. One day after the church service on Sunday night he came to the building. I was dismissing the people and helping the people get into the van. He showed up at the outside of the church door. He said, 'You're the pastor, aren't you?' I said, 'Yes.'

He said, 'Pastor, I need to talk to you.' He said, 'I'm the biggest drug dealer in the entire area. I'm dying with aids. I've got one question for you. I just have to know, will God forgive me?'

I took him to Isaiah 1:18 'Come now let us reason together. Though your sins be as scarlet, they shall be as white as snow. Though they be red like crimson, they shall be as wool.'

We knelt down on the front row of the church. I said, 'Why don't you ask God for forgiveness because God is willing to reason with you and forgive you.'

He knelt down at a chair on the front row and wept his way to Jesus."—Pastor Daniel McCrillis

GRACE BAPTIST CHURCH

This burden began as the Highway 30 Corridor Church Initiative. The very first meetings were held in the fall of 2003 in a private home off Highway 30 in House Springs, Missouri. This was in the form of a Bible Study held on Thursday nights. I conducted these meetings, and taught the Bible. We tried to stir things in this area by taking the Gospel door to door.

We soon realized that a more concrete effort was needed and prayed much about the matter. We sought God much for His guidance on where and how we ought see this through.

God led us we believe to contact a friend in the ministry, a youth director named Jerry Ross who was an assistant pastor at Blessed Hope Baptist Church in Jasonville, Indiana. The plan was to involve two youth groups, ours at Arnold Baptist Tabernacle and the youth group at Blessed Hope.

At this time, I began to see the importance of the evangelist in the model. We contacted Evangelist Lou Difillipantonio and shared our plan. Our goal was twofold: 1. To bring encouragement to a new church in Farmington, Missouri (Blessed Hope Baptist

Church, named for Bro. Ross's church)[12] and 2. Hold a special service—a youth rally in House Springs, Missouri to act as a springboard for a new church.

The third week of July, 2004 was set for the bringing together of our youth groups along with Evangelist Difillipantonio. But the location of the Highway 30 plant was very much in the air.

As the date for our rally, Friday July 23, 2004 was very certain, our faith was tested for the exact location. This aspect we believed was not just important, but eminently vital. The closer we got to the date, the more determined we became to find the right place.

An old church building off Highway 30 and Upper Byrnes Mill Road became available. Through a miraculous set of circumstances, we were allowed to use this building for the cost of insurance (about $125.00 per month).

We were ready for the rally. The teens visited and 25-30 visiting young people came to the meeting. The families of these young guests were the first prospects of the sprouting church. We faithfully followed up on every one of them and continued to preach the Gospel to people house to house.

For a year I preached in the afternoon at the new work which we initially called Grace Independent Baptist Church. Of course I preached to our church in Arnold in the morning. My wife and I packed a lunch, put our younger children in our van immediately after church, and drove to the Highway 30 location at Grace.

We sang and preached at 2:00 pm. We always had a family or two from A.B.T. to come and sit as a church. We had a few people saved, and some people from the area started attending on a regular basis.

We asked the sprouting church to seek the guidance of God for a man to come and be their pastor. We were clueless on who this might be. But we prayed earnestly that God would send the right man.

A young evangelist Matt Dudley, who was originally from this part of the country, came to a camp meeting held at Arnold Baptist Tabernacle in January of 2005. I had asked from the pulpit for

---

12 This church was already forming under the leadership of Pastor Jeff Brady.

prayer for the new work on Highway 30. Brother Dudley and I spoke and we arraigned for him to come and preach at Grace.

The day he preached at Highway 30, the Lord so impressed upon my heart that he should come and take the work, I asked him to earnestly pray that God would send him. God honored that impression and that is exactly what happened.

Not long afterwards the church was formed under the leadership of Pastor Matt Dudley. They began to grow, and negotiated the purchase of the Highway 30 property. They grew out of the building, sold it and merged with a sister church in Catawissa, Missouri. The Grace Baptist Church of Catawissa, Missouri continues to grow and has plans to plant a new church in the near future.

Chapter 12
The Multiplying Model in Other Places

In order to encourage others to step out by faith and use the model, we now present testimony from other pastors. These testimonies are from churches in several states among churches of various sizes.

The testimony of Pastor Rocky Fritz, Pastor of the First Baptist Church of Amboy, Illinois on assisting in the planting of Heritage Baptist Church in Princeton, Illinois:

"We've been at our church for a number of years, and felt the Lord wanted us to plant a church. We were actually considering leaving the church and starting a church somewhere on our own. We were introduced to the concept of church planting the old Baptist way by evangelist Ted Alexander. Through the influence of studying the Separate Baptist movement, we decided it would be best to stay where we were and out of our church plant other churches in the surrounding communities. There are a number of communities around us (we live in a very small town of 2,400) and there are a number of communities around us that are 2 or 3 times our size.

We saw that Princeton, Illinois was a place that did not have an independent Baptist Church. We felt like that would be a good place to start. It was close enough to drive back and forth on Sundays and hold services. It was far enough that we weren't going to reach people from that community by our church.

We found a building to meet in and just went down on Sunday afternoons and held services. Basically our morning service, we just re-did it. We brought different people from the church each Sunday. So we had some workers there people to greet visitors, nursery workers, whatever was needed including musicians. We found an outstanding building in which we were able to meet, a community center. They didn't charge us anything for it, so it was a real blessing. It really didn't cost us anything to start other than the time invested for services on Sunday and soul winning on Saturday afternoons.

Usually I would go and preach. I would just re-preach my Sunday morning message. We made the service a little bit shorter. After we

46

had been there for awhile, we started using different men to preach.

We really had thought from the beginning our assistant pastor would go there to pastor the church. So we started to use him to do some of the preaching. When it got to where we had a Sunday morning service, he went.

We had a few people who were very interested from the start that we met just going out knocking on doors. A couple of them drove quite a distance to the church that they were attending. We talked to their pastor and got to know him. He was all for them going somewhere closer.

We met on Sunday afternoon for probably a little more than a year. A lot of folks had made comments that if we had Sunday morning services they would come, Sunday afternoon was an inconvenient time for some for a church service. We felt it was time to make that move. Really by faith we just said, "Ok, we will switch to Sunday morning, which meant our assistant pastor left our services.

Once he started Sunday morning church, they really picked up quickly. They met for a couple of months and had enough people interested and had a charter service.

They were still meeting in the community building when a church building became available, an evangelical church was moving. This was an old church building—many different churches have used it. It was available for a very good price, so they purchased the building. We ordained our assistant to become the pastor, and they voted him in as pastor.

It was a very exciting thing for the people of our church to be involved. From the very beginning there was a lot of enthusiasm about it. Our church is a very old church; this is the first time any one of us has been involved in anything like it.

 Giving birth to a church is a struggle for a church, but its well worth it in the long run. Our people have become stronger through it and we're really praying about doing this again."

—Pastor Rocky Fritz

The testimony of Pastor Joe Esposito, Pacific Baptist Church in Long Beach, California on assisting in the planting of Pacific Baptist Church in Los Angeles, California:

"As we studied the book of Acts, we knew God wanted us to be involved in church planting. We saw many different models. We talked to many different preachers.

About 2 years ago we were introduced to the history of church planting in America.

Churches planted churches. Some of the people (sometimes called "sitters," sometimes called other names)—a hand full of families—participate in the new church as it starts.

In this way you can have some greeters; you can have people that are actually singing from the very first service. You can have people that love God in the services. Loving God is contagious. That is what we did. Our people, our church started a church 18 miles away.

Our people would go out on Tuesday nights. We had people sign up to say who would go out from our church to go plant a church, to do some soul winning, go do some door knocking, go invite people to the brand new church. We started it.

Because of circumstances, we only had about 3 months to prepare. We obtained a building. The first Sunday to our surprise, there were almost 300 people in attendance. A number of people were saved. Of course 300 people were not there the next Sunday, but because we had our people from our church helping, we were able to keep a lot more than if that we had helped some fellow 200 miles away and gave him a love offering or even monthly support. He may have had 300 people on that first Sunday, but there would be no one to follow-up. In our case, we had some workers. Every Sunday, even up until this day, we have had workers sitting as a church helping the church plant. Those workers are training other workers. They are teaching new converts. They are training wayward Christians that were invited to that new local church. We are trying to train up leaders in the new church now.

I believe since January of 2010, the average attendance in the church plant is 170. Just having the people from our church, having the workers is huge.

We go back to what we were introduced to about 2 years ago. Bro. Beller came to our church and introduced us to something we had never heard before, and it is phenomenal. I would encourage any pastor to catch the vision, study the history. Ask the Lord to clarify the plan to start churches, and do it the old Baptist way.

I am pastoring the new church right now. Again, because our church has planted a church, it is our baby. We don't have a pastor as of yet.

Of course there's some travail there. But the blessing of having a little baby cannot compare to all the work and the travail. So what we did was push our service times back. We pushed our Sunday School back 30 minutes. We have Sunday School at 9:30 am and at 10:30 I preach at our morning service. I hand the invitation over to my brother. I have a car out in front of the church waiting for me. My son is there. He drives me to the church plant. It is an easy drive. There is no traffic. We get there usually in less than 20 minutes. They've already had congregational singing. They usually have already had the offering. I get there and I preach. I will stay there until the last person is gone. God has given us the grace and strength. But again we have the help of the home church. We are all working it together. There is spiritual Baptist energy working.

The people in Monterey Park that we are reaching are a part of an international community. These folks all speak English, but they are all different nationalities. There are new people getting saved, wayward Christians that have not been in church for years that are looking for a church, trying to find something that is best for their family.

Our people are so excited. I am convinced it will be very easy to start the next church plant."

—Pastor Joe Esposito

Chapter 13
The Stages of the Multiplying Model

What are the stages in planting a church using the scriptural and historic model of the Separate Baptists?

No two church plants are alike, but we believe there are definite steps after which we may pattern the work. How is it accomplished?

If we turn to the book of Acts for our pattern we may be a bit overwhelmed. The church at Jerusalem was a miracle church, unusual in every way. The church was huge no doubt about it, but it is evident that God allowed it to be scattered. In the dispersion of its membership, the people of God went everywhere and preached the Gospel. Later the Apostle Paul as an evangelist gathered many of those scattered people into churches. He also furthered the Gospel by his own preaching to the lost.

We believe our search for a scriptural and historical model for church planting takes us to the Apostle Paul. Obviously, Paul lived in obedience to the Great Commission found in Matthew 28:19-20, a commission which included preaching the Gospel to every creature, baptizing believers into the local church, and teaching them. Paul even reveals what he taught these new believers in their new churches in Hebrews 6:1-2.

It is evident also in the ministry of the Apostle Paul that the time required to bring a church to fruition greatly increased from the time of the miracle at Jerusalem. We would all like to think our church could grow into the thousands in a matter of weeks, but it just does not happen. This did not happen for the Apostle Paul, either. He ministered for various amounts of time in different places. He travailed, which means he *agonized* with people again and again.

With travail in mind we may think of church planting in a metaphor somewhat like the growth of a plant. We might say there is a **determination stage**, a **sowing stage**, a **sprouting stage**, and finally, the **fruition stage**. If each stage is done decently and in order, you should have a living church as a result.

DETERMINATION STAGE

By correctly sowing a new work and guarding its ordinances, you will build a strong foundation. A new church needs to be launched correctly. We contend there are basically two ways to launch a new church.

One, a church planter, (evangelist or missionary) is sent from an existing church to a remote location for the task of planting a new church. **Two**, an established pastor launches a new church in close proximity to his own existing sowing church. The sowing church aids directly in the work. The results on the island of Crete illustrate number two. Crete could not have been accomplished without Titus physically doing the work of an evangelist.

The first stage of any church plant is DETERMINATION. Determination is exemplified by the Apostle Paul on the backside of the desert walking with God and receiving instruction directly from the Lord Jesus Christ. The pastor of the existing church has to make a determination. He has to find the will of God. The church planter also has to make a determination. An evangelist also should be praying. In this stage of church planting we must walk with God and determine what God wants us to do.

1. Pray.
2. Empty yourself of any desire.
3. Study areas.
4. Look for a call to a specific area.
5. Determine to work your way through.
6. Prepare your church by connecting them to their history.

Let us discuss preparing your church for a moment. History is what happened. Heritage is what we do with history. Obadiah Holmes made history by resisting the control of the Congregational church establishment. When we learn by his example and resist tyranny by obeying God rather than man, we are living our heritage.

Give the people of your church their Baptist history. Use illustrations drawn from the experiences of Shubal Stearns, Daniel

51

Marshall, John Waller and Samuel Harriss.[13] For instance, I spoke of Harriss repeatedly up to the time of asking our church to participate in the first church plant. When your men hear stories of men of this caliber, it makes them want to do something for the Lord. It creates a desire to lead.

7. Determine to work your way through.

8. If able, raise some money, but don't bank on it.

9. Don't take too much time preparing or your people may lose interest.

10. Use a special service to introduce the burden and the plan to plant churches.

Below is an invite card we sent to our church family announcing that missionary Jim Beller (yes that is me) was coming to the church to share his burden. Our people were intrigued by this and came with expecting hearts.

This Sunday Night
at the Tabernacle!
MISSIONARY JIM BELLER
will be sharing his burden for his mission
field * Don't miss this!
Meet his family! * Come expecting to
hear from God.

THIS SUNDAY NIGHT SEPTEMBER 21, 1997 8 PM
ARNOLD BAPTIST TABERNACLE
3706 TELEGRAPH ROAD
ARNOLD, MO. 63010-PH:464-7066

A slide presentation explaining the Separate Baptist model was shown. We laid out the history of the model and presented a plan including: working together in prayer, supporting your pastor, financing together, supporting housing, supporting location for a new church, supporting through grocery money and sitting as a church. There were pictures in the presentation. There was music. There was an invitation to do something. This meeting knit our hearts together as we determined to start some churches together.

SOWING STAGE

---

13 For these illustrations see the author's book, *America in Crimson Red*, Chapters 7-14.

In this stage of the new church progress can be readily seen or frustratingly invisible. Preaching, public services, Bible studies, Sunday meetings, etc. are held to meet people, see them saved, and to disciple them.

In this stage we taught doctrine, Baptist distinctives, and the simple Gospel message. Explain to all interested parties the intention is to plant a new church.

Here are some other suggestions for the **sowing stage**:

1. **Pray and search out a place to meet.** Your goal is zero out-of pocket expense. (See Chapter 17 on *Ideas.*) Find a location for your first series of meetings. This could be anywhere. Again, we have a goal that the beginning place should be at no cost or close to it. Twice we have met in living rooms and at other times we borrowed church buildings or abandoned church buildings.

2. **In this stage we sow and we sow abundantly.** Talk to everybody, hand out tracts and flyers to everybody, and try to meet as many people as possible. Get the word of God into the hands of as many people as possible.

3. **Organize the sowing church with sign-up sheets** for taking the Gospel and invitations to the new area. Sign them up to sit as a church. Eventually they should be led to sign-up for grocery money for the new pastor. Start with afternoon sits and work into Sunday morning with the new pastor.

4. **Distribute large numbers of tracts and flyers**. Go door-to-door and talk to as many folks as possible.

5. **Initiate with a special meeting(s).** We usually started with Bible studies, youth rallies or something similar. In the sowing stage your goal is simply to meet people. Anything in this stage that causes you to meet people and give them the Gospel is good for sowing. For us the ideal start was Sunday afternoon meetings in an inexpensive place.

6. **Prepare yourself for the time it takes.** The church planting pastor who does the work of an evangelist will need to set aside time for sowing. We have devoted Saturday afternoons for this task and we have always been able to find people.

7. The key is enlist a handful of people (it doesn't take a large number) involved in the sowing stage. They need to be positive and very energetic. It is a great opportunity for young people, and we have found that they absolutely love it.

I cannot tell you how long the sowing stage will continue. It could be just a few months or it may be a period of years as it was with the Apostle Paul at Ephesus. Remember you are trying to gather materials to begin a new church. It is going to take some time. Do not worry if the results are slow for quite some time.

We preached in the sowing stage at the Grace Independent Baptist Church plant for well over a year. In South St. Louis, we held afternoon services for over a year and saw no one saved. But we were always convinced that we were in the right place and since not a lot of money was spent in sowing, we were able to continue on with little pressure.

8. Preach Christ, or teach through basic books such as Romans Galatians and Ephesians.

9. In the sowing stage, those baptized in the new church are technically members of the established or sowing church. This is because the new church is a ministry of the existing church. We believe this to be the safest and most scriptural way.

Consider yourself in the sowing stage until you have three to four families that appear to be committed to the cause of the new church.

SPROUTING STAGE

When the Lord has given you three or four families who show real interest in the work, you are transitioning into what I refer to as the **sprouting stage**.

1. In the sprouting stage, center all of your messages on Jesus. Do not give personal illustrations. Use Bible illustrations or use illustrations from Baptist history. This will help a sprouting church gain its unique identity as an independent Baptist congregation.

2. If you are not in a more permanent place by now, earnestly seek one.

3. Make the services more like fully fledged church and take advantage of those who sit as a church by using them to help.

4. Train them to take the Gospel to others.

5. The established pastor, doing the work of an evangelist, should not become too close to the people of the new church. Do not capture their hearts to yourself. You are leading them to accept another shepherd. This is absolutely necessary because you will need to be relieved of this duty to care for your primary flock. Additionally, you need to be free to do this work once again.

Remind the people that you are a missionary and that sometime soon the Lord will provide a man of God for the new work. Lead the people to pray at this time for the right man to come and take it. Until this time, the missionary evangelist has done the preaching, teaching, and basic work of a pastor. The people who are gathered need to know what must transpire. God's man for that church must come. They must pray, seeking God's will for the mission church. The best case scenario would be someone you personally trained, perhaps one of your own preacher boys. Whoever it is, it has to be the man of God's choosing and no one else.

We never campaigned for a preacher to come. But in normal conversations with our friends, other preachers, and in meetings we would simply ask others to pray about the situation.

There was a time when "licensing" a preacher was akin to the "exhorter" concept of the Separate Baptists. A licensed preacher can preach, but not administer the ordinances. The time of exhorting can serve as an internship in which a man can be proved before he is ordained. Certainly this would lower the failure rate.

Pray earnestly about the man of God's choosing. Consider this story: In Charleston, South Carolina in the days following the Civil War, the famous First Baptist Church was devastated. It had but a handful of members left from its once mighty congregation, and had lost its pastor during the days of the suffering of the confederacy.

Prayer was offered by what was left of the congregation on a weekly basis. They would meet in the partially boarded up building praying on the platform, begging God to send His man to resurrect the work.

One day a preacher felt led of God to travel to Charleston. His mission was to visit the churches in the devastated area hoping he might be a help to any scattered Baptist Christians. He prayed that the Lord might lead him to the right place—a place where he would be needed most.

One night he rode on horseback down the avenue leading to the First Baptist Church. He came along the side of the building where the windows had been boarded. He did not know it, but inside the building at that exact moment the people of the church were pleading with God for leadership.

As he leaned against a boarded up window, the board cracked and he crashed through the window onto the platform where the people where praying. The surprised members stood up from their prayers and asked who he was. When he informed them of his mission they knew immediately that their prayers had been answered and that man became their pastor!

God knows where His men are and where they need to be. Rather than having a list of prerequisites and counting on applications pray that a man of like minded faith and fervency will be found for the fledgling congregation.

In many cases when God sends the right man, it will become his job to charter the church and declare its independence.

6. Receive offerings. This will offset what is hoped will be a small amount of rent. Money could be saved for the needs of the fruition stage.

FRUITION STAGE

Eventually the church will transition into what we refer to as the **fruition stage**. Here are some characteristics of this stage:

1. When the church has reason to believe it can stand on its own financially and spiritually, it ought to be formed or publically declared as a church.

2. Can the bills be paid to simply operate?

3. Are the people grounded in the word of God so they may generally repel apostasy?

4. Are the people mature enough to preach the Gospel, teach

converts and bring them into fellowship?
    5. Are the people willing to take responsibly the duties of prayer, watching for their church family, tithing, discipline, and testimony?
    6. Is God leading them to form as a church?

We believe a church is brought into existence when a group of regenerate people, united by proper doctrines of the nature of God and salvation, and having proper baptism are led by the Spirit of God to publicly declare themselves an independent church. This would coincide with all of the members dismissed from the established or sowing church to the new church. The church would then operate alone under the rule of Christ.

The independent Baptist church would then as led by God, extend a call to the new pastor. In other words the church would publicly declare what God had already done in their midst. In order to do things decently and in order they should declare the visitation of God by written methods stating plainly their doctrines and intents. This could be done by means of a charter service where the members sign a public declaration.

Chapter 14
Some Things for Which to Prepare

Early in 2010 as we were finishing this manuscript, we received this letter:

Pastor Beller,

My father-in-law, Pastor xxxxx xxxxxx, is on staff at xxxxxxx Baptist Church. He was just with us two weekends ago and told me a lot about you.

My wife and I are currently serving at xxxxx Baptist Church in xxxxx xxxxxxxx I've been on staff here as an intern for four years with the goal of being sent out to plant a church.

Pastor xxxxxxx had mentioned that you have planted multiple churches and have a great heart for seeing your area reached with the gospel.

If you could give me some insight as to the steps you take in planting a church.
- Choosing of a location.
- Budgeting for the new plant .
- Long range strategic planning of planting more churches.
- Process leading up to start date.

Our heart is to settle into a suburb of a metro area and plant a church with the long range plan of starting multiple other churches from that one just as you have in your case.

I'd love to get some feedback from you. We are excited but understanding this is a process led by the Lord.

Thanks for your time!

xxxxx xxxxxx

I hope that most of these questions have been covered in this book. I would like to make a few more observations.
- **Choosing a location.** Remember, this is not arbitrary. It must be the place of God's choosing. Do your research, but let your tears fall on a map as you seek God's guidance. Do not be guilty of simply closing your eyes and putting your finger on a map.
- **Budgeting for the new plant.** If the church planter is going to a

remote location, he should be supported somewhat. But I would challenge a young man to go to the area of God's choosing and work a job. We did this for the first three years. Why should other churches take a chance on you or any other young man and throw away thousands of dollars when you quit? Let us return to our model. With a sowing church launching out, and/or coming along side a church planter, less money is needed, more faith is exercised.

A budget is based on your income. The budget divides your income into percentages. Those percentages cannot be breached. Go for inexpensive or zero-out-of-pocket locations. Live in someone's basement. Borrow a mobile home. We lived in a two-room backhouse that belonged to my aunt. Go cheap. Plan the cost of tracts, fliers, and brochures.

- **Long-range strategic planning.** After you have established a strong church, drive, pray, talk to people, get your map out and weep until you get a leading. If every pastor had this vision we could help our country.
- **Process leading up to the start date.** See Determination Stage from Chapter 13, along with other info scattered throughout this book.

Chapter 15
The Don'ts of the Multiplying Model

Often in discussing with fellow pastors the subject of the multiplying model of church planting, there are misconceptions that fill the conversation. Many pastors shy away from the idea of planting a church for fear of the intangibles involved. For instance, many pastors fear that somehow planting a church will hurt their established church. Others feel it will cost a tremendous amount of money. Whatever the fear is, it really is an excuse not to take the Great Commission to its proper conclusion. Here are a few *don'ts* that should clear up a few misconceptions regarding the multiplying model.

1. Don't choose on simple need. Do not attempt a church plant just because it looks like it is a good idea. This needs to be a result of extended, fervent prayer. While you may see a desperate need somewhere, do not arbitrarily pick a place.

Jesus gave us an example of this. When the disciples toiled all night and caught nothing, the Lord simply told them to cast their nets on the other side of the boat. It was a good idea to fish, it was even a good place to fish, but they were not fishing where Jesus wanted them. Sometimes a church plant will fail simply because everybody but Jesus thought it was a good idea.

When Shubal Stearns headed south on his mission, it was after many months of prayer. His first stop was in Virginia where he prayed for quite some time before receiving a definite call to North Carolina. Daniel Marshall had a similar experience in that he first journeyed to Pennsylvania where he and his wife Martha first attempted to win the Indians to Christ. Further prayer directed them to Virginia to meet-up with Stearns and head south to North Carolina. These prayerful moves resulted in the fruitful ministry which became Sandy Creek Baptist Church and Association.

Do not open a map and arbitrarily put your finger on some place. Open a map, put in on the floor, get on your knees and pray until you get a definite leading.

2. Don't just raise money for a new work, support a true

evangelist. I have been in meetings where church planting has been emphasized and the sole purpose for the meeting was to raise money for the church planter. We are not opposed to this; however, if we are using the multiplying model and the established pastor is doing the work of an evangelist, then in many cases, not a whole lot of money is needed to plant the church.

The established pastor either launches out himself or comes along side the church planter. The evangelist in our model comes along side the church planter and ought to be supported so that he may stay for an extended time to preach the Gospel and gather souls into the new church.

The Separate Baptists birthed 1,000 churches in 20 years without the aid of a single millionaire. They established nearly 5,000 new churches in 40 years without the aid of any financial organization. They went out by faith, they preached the Gospel by faith, and they gathered churches by faith.

So often we try to raise money for that which God wants to finance supernaturally. John Taylor, the great evangelist to the state of Kentucky, raised no funds and managed to plant over 30 churches in that land. Samuel Harriss, the *Apostle of Virginia*, did similar work, planting over 50 churches in that state alone. All of this was done without raising large sums of money. This was true of hundreds of Separate Baptist pioneer preachers.

3. Don't institutionalize this ministry. The multiplying ministry of church planting belongs to the local New Testament church. Man-made institutions such as colleges, foundations, boards, associations, trust funds, etc., do not plant churches. So why institutionalize this logical conclusion of the Great Commission?

Why is it that when God gives a local church a fruitful ministry, is there an effort to somehow institutionalize it across the country? The planting of churches should be a natural progression from existing churches and should be nurtured and financed through each particular assembly. Stop thinking like a liberal politician who throws money at a problem, just get out and do it in obedience to the Great Commission.

4. Don't expect to be beloved. Consider the experience of the

Apostle Paul in 2 Timothy 1:15, "This thou knowest, that all they which are in Asia be turned away from me; of whom are Phygellus and Hermogenes."

You will probably not become the "beloved sage" of your region. Forget about the accolades from the lips of men, that behavior is what ails us today.

Chapter 16
Review of the Four Factors of Success

We gave you these four factors back in Chapter 1. We repeat them here for emphasis. The four factors are:

1. Strong pastoral leadership. The pastor of the sowing church is the missionary in this model. Without his leadership, effort, burden, and belief there is no hope for success.

2. Participation by the sowing church membership. The sowing church must be squarely behind the work. It is they, the families that must participate—not committees, college students or professional teams.

3. The right man to pastor the new work. He has to be called to that location. He has to be a God-called man, sent by God.

4. The right location. Supernatural direction is needed for the model.

The multiplying model will fail for lack of any of these factors.

Chapter 17
Ideas

1. Have a Special Meeting to Gather Souls. This purpose of this idea is to find prospective members for the new church. Go, meet people, give them the Gospel and invite them to the special meeting.

In the following example our church planned a church planting week of visitation which involved our teens. We invited another teen group to help us and we planned for visiting and inviting young people to a youth rally on a Friday night. Here was our schedule:

Church Planting Week
July 20-23, 2004

Welcome

Welcome the Blessed Hope Baptist Church youth group under the direction of Bro. Jerry Ross.

Welcome also Bro. Lou Difillipantonio from Grace Baptist Church in Gaylord, Michigan.

The Two Churches and our purpose...

Farmington, Missouri

The Blessed Hope Baptist Church was birthed into existence on July 18, 2004. It's a body church pastored by Bro. Jeff Brady.

Our purpose is to saturate Farmington with information about the new church by putting flyers and tracts on every door and into the hands of every person we meet. We will do this by covering a quarter of the city each day.

House Springs

The Grace Independent Baptist Church is to hold its first service July 25, 2004 at 2:00 p.m.

Our purpose this week is to cover the Highway 30 corridor with flyers and invite teens to a youth rally to be held Friday at 7:00 p.m. We will ask you to "sign-up" prospects and hand out flyers and tracts. The families the teens represent will be the first prospects of the new church. If it is feasible to win the teen to Christ, do so.

TUESDAY JULY 20, 2004
1:00 pm Opening assembly at Arnold Baptist Tabernacle. Pastor Beller, Bro. Difillipantonio
1:30 - 5:00 visitation
5:00 Supper at the Grace Independent Baptist Church, House Springs provided by ABT
5:45-7:30 Fix-up time
7:45 Mini service. Pastor Beller Q and A and prayer.

WEDNESDAY JULY 21, 2004
10:00 am Opening assembly devotions
10:30 - 12:00 noon visitation
12:00 Lunch provided by ABT
12:30 - 3:00 Visitation
6:00 pm Supper at Arnold Baptist Tabernacle
7:15 Church at ABT

THURSDAY JULY 22, 2004
10:00 am Opening Assembly
10:30-12 noon visitation
12:00 Lunch provided by ABT
12:30-2:00 visitation
3:00 meet back at ABT
4:00-?? River boat cruise and dinner on board (cost $15.00-17.00)

FRIDAY JULY 23, 2004
10:00 am Opening Assembly
10:30-12:00 noon visitation
12:00 Lunch provided by ABT
12:30-2:30 visitation
2:30-3:30 organize call backs
4:00 Supper at the Grace Independent Baptist Church, House Springs provided by ABT
5:00-7:00 call back and pick up
7:00 Rally at Grace Independent Baptist Church

Since we were also visiting to help a church which had just had its opening service, we canvassed in support of that new work, and at the same time worked toward the special teen rally for the brand new church. We hoped to meet some people that may be the core of a new church, specifically the families of some of the teens that would attend the youth rally.

We brought in an evangelist to be better organized and divided the teens into two groups and assigned group leaders. The responsibilities of the group leaders are shown below:

Church planting week July 20-23, 2004

Responsibilities of the team leader...

1. Prayer for teammates.

2. The spirit of your team.

3. Bus program for Farmington trips approx 45 minutes.
     a)singing
     b)preaching
     c)games
     d)testimonies
     e)teaching talk to Bro. D. or Bro. Beller

4. You need to assign a "chow crew" consisting of three young ladies from your team. They will take care of the mobile lunches and help serve the suppers.

5. Make sure your team is in the right place at the right time and has the right tools.
     a)flyers
     b)tracts
     c)prospect cards
     d)pens
     e)cleaning or fix up supplies

     Bro. Beller's cell phone: 314-606-7326

We met each morning for instruction and encouragement. We gave prospect cards to the workers. A copy of the prospect card is on the next page.

Grace Independent Baptist Church contact card   *Date:* _____

Name:

Address:

Phone:

email:

Comments:

Blessed Hope Baptist Church contact card   *Date:* _____

Name:

Address:

Phone:

email:

Comments:

After the special meeting was concluded we then distributed a general flyer for the new church:

Grace Independent Baptist Church

Our services are held Sunday afternoon's at 2:00 P.M.

3774 Hess Road, House Springs, MO 63051

Yes, we are that beautiful church at the corner of
Hiway 30 and Upper Byrnes Mill.
Call 314-606-7326 for more information

Bring your family and friends and join in on the miracle beginning
of a New Testament Church!

2. Tent or Revival Meetings. Tent or revivals are good ways to meet people and stir up a community. Many evangelists have tents and have used them to great advantage.

3. Saving Money. I hope you understand by now that while buildings, materials, song books, advertising, etc. are important, they are not entirely necessary for the model to work. A local church can pool its resources and influences to bring about the planting of another church. Here are some tips:

a) Find an unused building or use a building at a time when no one else is using it.

b) Use a motel meeting room. It is amazing how inexpensive this can be especially if you tell the owner/manager it will be used on Sunday afternoon over an extended period. Negotiate a less expensive price because of the fact you will be using it for 6 to 12 months or more.

c) Use the living room of an interested person. This was done twice in our experience. It is a good idea during the sowing stage.

d) In a more rural setting, township halls are often available and usually at no cost.

4. Here is an example progression in a church plant:

a) Door to door to compile and collect information.

b) Re-contact to conduct one on one Bible studies.

c) After a period of time, special meetings are conducted with contacts together. (Under a tent or something similar.)

d) Begin Sunday services.

Postscript
Imagine
The Shubal Stearns Initiative

Shubal Stearns was 55 years of age when he started his ministry in North Carolina. Daniel Marshall was 65 when he began his extraordinary work in the state of Georgia. Jeremiah Vardemann organized a church two days before his death in Missouri. The multiplying model was a way of life for them. It could be implemented at any time and at any age.

Imagine this. There are roughly 14,000 independent Baptist churches throughout America. Using the Separate Baptist model, if those churches could birth just one church, it would bring 14,000 new churches into existence. Imagine if those new churches grew to a very modest 100 in membership. It would mean 1.4 million more Americans would be in a Bible preaching Baptist church! Is this not *revival*?

Pastor, do the work of an evangelist.

Evidence suggests much better success in church planting if we bring pastors, church planters and evangelists together.
**Visit the Shubal Stearns Initiative, and the
Great Commission Coalition at
www.multiplyingmodel.com**